Millie

W9-BTZ-707

Very Rare
GLASSWARE
of the Depression Years
Fourth Series

Gene Florence

COLLECTOR BOOKS

A Division of Schroeder Publishing Co., Inc.

The current values in this book should be used only as a guide. They are not intended to set prices, which vary from one section of the country to another. Auction prices as well as dealer prices vary greatly and are affected by condition as well as demand. Neither the Author nor the Publisher assumes responsibility for any losses that might be incurred as a result of consulting this guide.

Other Books by Gene Florence

On the cover:
Jubilee three footed bowl, Sunrise Medallion blue pitcher, Caribbean blue oyster cocktail.

Additional copies of this book may be ordered from:

COLLECTOR BOOKS
P.O. Box 3009
Paducah, KY 42002-3009
or
Gene Florence
P.O. Box 22186
Lexington, KY 40522

@$24.95. Add $2.00 for postage and handling.

Copyright: Gene Florence, 1995

This book or any part thereof may not be reproduced without the written consent of the Author and Publisher.

Printed by IMAGE GRAPHICS, INC., Paducah, Kentucky

Contents

The reception of the three previous editions of <u>Very Rare Glassware of the Depression Years</u> has been "awesome" to quote my son, Marc. I had wondered if collectors would respond to a "coffee table" book of rarely seen and "hard to find" items. My first series of <u>Very Rare</u> has already been reprinted three times and one of the limited (500) leather bound copies recently sold for $145. That price is rapidly approaching the price of my first edition <u>Collector's Encyclopedia of Depression Glassware</u>. As an author who loves his work, I thank you, my readers, for all the wonderful letters and phone calls asking when another <u>Very Rare Glassware of the Depression Years</u> would be available; thus, I introduce you to the fourth series.

As with most books, a later edition is easier to do than the first one. The most troublesome decision is to establish a format that is simple enough yet usable for novices and advanced collectors alike. After that, all that remains is finding enough rarely seen items for another book! As before, I am only showing rare pieces that encompass the time period and patterns shown in my Depression Era books and my <u>Collectible Glassware from the 40's, 50's, 60's</u>.

Obtaining glassware was easier this time since after seeing the earlier books many collectors approached me to advise me of their treasures. (Several have found that photography of glassware is not an easy task and lent me the glass for my photographer to capture their prized possessions. Someday I will have to write a book about my adventures in borrowing collector's rare glassware, and then photographing and searching for said photographs when they are finally needed three or four years later.) Some pieces that were to be included in this edition unfortunately were put on hold until next time since book deadlines arrived before I could find the missing pictures. That makes a fast start for the next book. Without your keeping watch for unknown glassware, I could never have found enough to put this book together in the mere two years that this edition took! Thanks!

A few photographs for this book were taken over a four year period. I was not able to include some pieces in the last book so they were carried over to this one. After newly discovered items or unusual colors of commonly found pieces were discovered, I had them photographed at the earliest opportunity. This sounds simple enough, but when you are dealing with several photographers, and with thousands of prints/transparencies, and with a publisher and editor with hundreds of books in the works, even after shots are taken and approved, photographs sometimes end up missing! (This time we even have the test photos, {Polaroid}, of one item that never did show up in a final print when it was needed.) Too, it is difficult to get some pieces to show both color and pattern; and sometimes it takes two or three photography sessions to obtain satisfactory results with a piece. Even that never seemed to solve the problem of locating the right print when you needed it! Was it still at the photographers, photo lab, printers, the publishers, the author's home in Florida or in his business files in Kentucky? Believe me, some photographs I need are always where I am not!

Rare glass continues to be found as late as June, 1994! Several photographs shown in this book were of items discovered as late as June and photographed as late as July to be included in this book. Keep looking; maybe you will find some! (I know of three Heisey Zircon pieces that sold in June at a garage sale for $1.75 and there was at least a 20,000% gain made on that investment. Can you do that with stocks?!) A few items shown in the earlier books have now surfaced in previously unknown quantities. All of these were quickly bought and placed in collections! What will it be this time? There is a quick and ready market for rarely seen pieces. Glass enthusiasts hope that a similar abundance will occur with some of the items shown in this book.

I am confident this book can help you find some rare glass. Let me know; maybe you will uncover some pieces we can use in the next book!

Acknowledgments

Many collectors have allowed their rare glass to be photographed for this book, and each is acknowledged with the items shown. However, several collectors went beyond lending glass to be shown. A special thanks to Dick and Pat Spencer who brought not only their glass, but the glass of several other collectors from Illinois and Missouri. Bill and Lottie Porter, with grandson Quinten Keech, came all the way from Michigan with Lottie's glass. All of these fine folks helped unpack and repack their prized glassware for photography so that you could see the rarest Depression Era glassware that can be found. I also need to make note of the numerous pieces of glassware pictured that were provided by Dan Tucker and Lorrie Kitchen. Not only did they bring glassware to my house when traveling, but they also shipped my purchases to Paducah for me when I flew to shows as a guest. If it were not for these special people who are willing to share their collections with others, a book of this magnitude would be nearly impossible to do.

Photography was done by Richard Walker, Charley Lynch and Kenn Whitmyer. Assisting in layouts at the photography sessions from Collector Books were Sherry Kraus and Lisa Stroup. Jane White was lured back to help even though she no longer is employed by Collector Books.

Family has always been important to me in my work. Mom, "Grannie Bear," had helped pack and kept lists of all the pieces we had stored for photography for a big part of this book. Her death last year caused Cathy and me to have to work even harder to get this all together. Sons Chad and Marc helped me move glass as well as load and unload it for photography trips. Cathy, my wife, continues to be my editor, packer, proofreader and everlasting organizer. She attempts to put my varied written ideas into an intelligible form for the public. She and her mother, Sibyl, take several weeks, lots of tables and several rooms of the house to do most of the packing and correlating of patterns of glass for the photography sessions. All this makes it easier for me to accomplish my tasks in putting these books before you. Please know how very much we appreciate readers and collectors' resources of glass catalogue sheets and purchasing information.

Many people work behind the scenes to put a book together. Much praise belongs to unseen workers who make this book into a usable format. Layout is vital. It is important to get picture and type sizes to fit and all horizontal photos and verticals to blend; and placing patterns alphabetically by company does create a layout problem or two! Michelle Dowling of Collector Books' editing department worked on the layouts and straightened out my errors. All headaches and other problems with photographs disappearing and deadlines being met were given to my editor, Lisa Stroup.

If I've overlooked someone, forgive me. It was not intentional. Please know I'm grateful for all your efforts. I could not have completed this book without your assistance!

AKRO AGATE COMPANY 1911–1951

Akro Agate Company was founded in Akron, Ohio, in 1911. They produced marbles and games there until for financial reasons the company moved to Clarksburg, West Virginia, in 1914. Clarksburg offered quality sand as well as a vast supply of cheap natural gas. These were the two most needed materials for making glass marbles.

World War I helped to establish the Akro Agate Company as a major force in the marble making industry. Until that war, the importing of marbles from Germany had kept Akro Agate a fledgling business. With the demise of European competition due to the war, Akro Agate was able to fortify itself in the field of marble making to the point that by the Depression years, they manufactured seventy-five percent of the marbles made in the United States.

A competitor, Master Marbles, cut into Akro's business when it hired some of the machine designers working at Akro. (Those machines had never been patented to keep others from getting information on making their own!) That was a fortuitous turning point for collectors. Because of losing business in the marble industry, Akro turned to making other objects out of the same material. Flower pots, planters and other utility items were made. After the Westite Glass Company burned in 1936, Akro obtained their moulds and made a strong line of these items that prospered until World War II. During the latter half of the 1930s, they made a line of children's doll dishes, tobacco accessory items (ash trays, match holders, powder jars, etc.) and other utilitarian lines using the same glass material that had been used so successfully in their marbles. The doll or "play" dishes became a major line when "metal" play dishes disappeared since that material was needed for the machines of war. As Akro Agate had prospered during W.W.I, they again prospered because of W.W.II.

Paradoxically, the doom of this little company was sealed at the end of the war, however, by the introduction of plastic doll dishes and increased competition from Japan. In 1951, Akro Agate was sold to Clarksburg Glass Company; and today, collectors search for that elusive trademark (crow flying through the letter A). Akro was a shortened form of "as a crow"!

From the collection of Kenn and Margaret Whitmyer

From the collection of Kenn and Margaret Whitmyer

*MISS AMERICA Forest Green child's set
– rare color and item*

Author's Collection

SCOTTY DOG transparent blue powder jar – rare color

CAMBRIDGE GLASS COMPANY 1902–1958

The Cambridge Glass Company was started in Cambridge, Ohio, in 1902. Glass was made there until 1958, except for a short period in 1954 to 1955 when the plant was closed. Today, there is a National Cambridge Collector's Club. A Cambridge Museum is operated by that club and located on Rt. 40E in Cambridge, Ohio.

The glass photographed in this section represents the patterns made during the 1930s to the 1950s that are most collected today. Collectors of Cambridge glass began collecting the glass by colors and decorations that were distinctly Cambridge. However, as more and more Depression glass collectors started to notice the finer handmade glassware from Cambridge, dinnerware lines and sets began to be gathered. Thus, a new standard of collecting was created and the prices started rising.

If you are interested in joining the National Cambridge Collectors Club, their address is:
National Cambridge Collectors, Inc.,
P.O. Box 416GF,
Cambridge, Ohio 43275
(Dues are $15.00 a year.)

The following pages show some of the rarest pieces of Cambridge known in the dinnerware lines, with emphasis on color rarities as well as unusual pieces.

Author's Collection

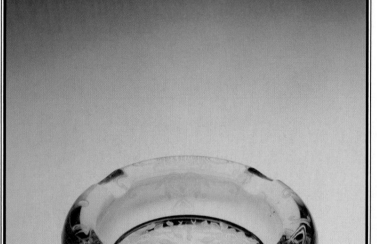

APPLE BLOSSOM Gold Krystol 6" ash tray – rare item

Author's Collection

APPLE BLOSSOM Amber #1066, 12 oz. sham bottom tumbler — rare item

Author's Collection

CLEO Emerald Green (light) Aero Optic 12" vase – rare item

Author's Collection

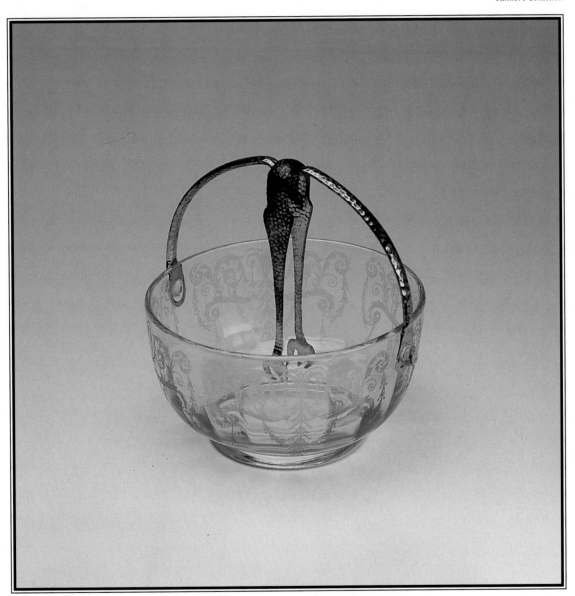

CLEO Willow Blue #3500/13 sugar basket – rare item

From the collection of Dan Tucker and Lorrie Kitchen

CLEO Willow Blue #1023, 9½" vase – rare item

From the collection of Earl and Beverly Hines

DIANE Peach-blo #3400 pitcher – rare color

Author's Collection

DIANE Crystal #498, 2 oz. bar glass

From the collection of Dan Tucker and Lorrie Kitchen

FORK and SPOON Cobalt blue #609 – rare color

Author's Collection

GLORIA Emerald green (light) pitcher – rare color

Author's Collection

GLORIA Emerald green (dark) #3400 pitcher – rare color

Author's Collection

PORTIA Emerald green (dark) #3400/54 cup – rare color

Author's Collection

Author's Collection

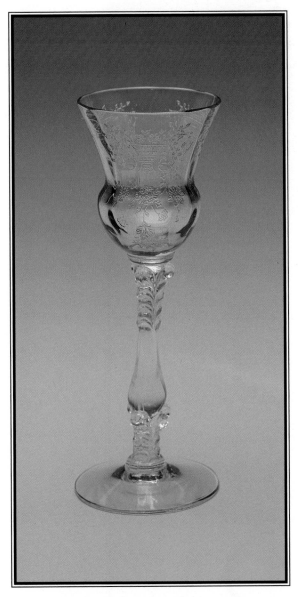

PORTIA Amber #3126 cordial – rare item

PORTIA Emerald green (dark) #3121 cordial – rare color

PORTIA Carmen gold encrusted #3035 cocktail — rare item

Author's Collection

ROSALIE Emerald green (light) seven part relish – rare item

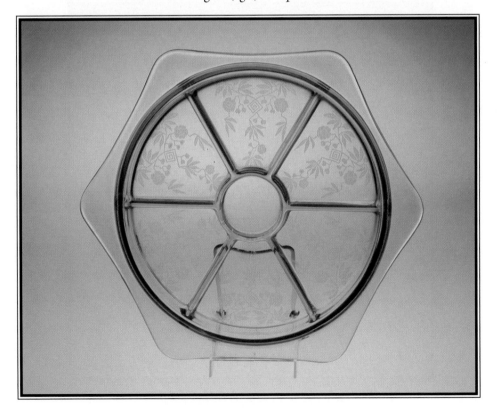

Author's Collection

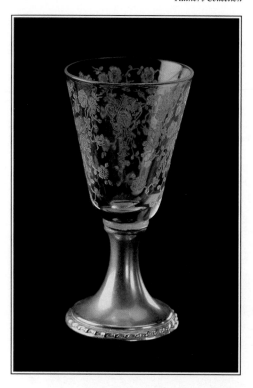

ROSE POINT Crystal #3106 cordial with Wallace Sterling base
– rare item

Author's Collection

ROSE POINT Cobalt pressed stem cordial

Author's Collection

ROSE POINT crystal Pristine 14" blown torte plate – rare item

Author's Collection

ROSE POINT crystal Pristine 3½" cocktail – rare item

From the collection of Swede and Kay Larsson

ROSE POINT Ebony gold encrusted 9" lamp – rare item

The new Duncan Miller Glass Company was incorporated in 1900 after beginning as the Duncan Glass Company in Pittsburgh and moving to Washington, Pennsylvania, in 1893. Although Duncan's glassware was not as widely distributed as some others, many collectors are seeking it today.

The patterns made during and shortly after the Depression years are in demand with collectors. One of the more popular patterns today is the Caribbean pattern made from 1936 until 1955. Although blue is the sought color, there are also those seeking the crystal.

Author's Collection

CARIBBEAN Blue oyster cocktail – rare item

FEDERAL GLASS COMPANY 1900-1984

Federal Glass Company was founded in Columbus, Ohio, and really prospered during the Depression with its dinnerware sets of Madrid, Patrician, Sharon and Parrot in colors of pink, blue, green and an amber known as "Golden Glo" in the patterns.

Federal became the first major company to reproduce a pattern from the Depression era with each piece marked. This "Recollection" pattern was copied from the original Madrid. It was issued in 1976 for the bicentennial and marked with '76 on each piece. These moulds were later sold to Indiana Glass Company and the '76 removed. Today, Indiana still makes this "Madrid-like" pattern in several colors and in pieces that were not originally made.

Author's Collection

GEORGIAN "Golden Glo" 6" sherbet plate – rare color
Although Federal's amber was the most predominate color used in this era,
this one piece of Georgian is all that has been seen in that color.

Author's Collection

PARROT Amber 5½", 10 oz., ftd. (Madrid mould) tumbler – rare item
These have yet to be found in green.

Author's Collection

PARROT Green 8½", 80 oz. pitcher - rare item
Originally, there were 37 of these found in the basement of an old hardware store in the early 1970's, but several of these have had accidents over the years.

Author's Collection

PARROT Green 4¼″ sherbet – rare item
There have been less than a dozen of these found.

Author's Collection

PATRICIAN Green cookie jar – rare color

From the collection of Iris Slayton

PATRICIAN Green vase – rare item
A cookie jar bottom was shaped into a vase by a factory worker. This was not a regular production item!

FENTON ART GLASS COMPANY *1907 to Present*

The first glassware was made at this plant in 1907 and it is still being made at the original site in Williamstown, West Virginia. Fenton made more Carnival and Art glass than they did glassware that is considered Depression ware. Lincoln Inn was one of their major patterns of the time, and the multitude of colors introduced in that line is astonishing. Begun in 1928, Lincoln Inn was made as late as the 1980s in an iridescent purple color.

Fenton Art Glass is still one of the few major glass companies that is continuing to operate in today's economy! Many gift shops and country stores carry Fenton's line and their adaptability to meet the public's demand for gift glassware has allowed them to continue to prosper in our ever changing world.

From the collection of Dan Tucker and Lorrie Kitchen

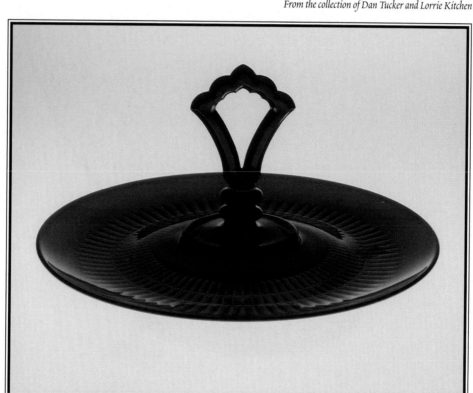

LINCOLN INN Cobalt blue center handled server – rare item

From the collection of Earl and Beverly Hines

LINCOLN INN Amber pitcher, 7¼", 46 oz. – rare item

Author's Collection

SILVER CREST White with crystal trim flat sugar and creamer – rare items

FOSTORIA GLASS COMPANY 1887–1986

Fostoria Glass Company almost survived a century! That included a major move from Fostoria, Ohio, to Moundsville, West Virginia, in the early days. Lancaster Colony bought Fostoria in the early 1980s but the glassware in the morgue at the factory was sold as late as December 1986.

The American pattern, first begun in 1915, was one of the longest made patterns in U.S. glass-making history! Lancaster Colony in continuing to make pieces available in this pattern through Indiana Glass Company and Dalzell Viking Glass Company.

Author's Collection

AMERICAN Opaque blue 6" bowl – rare color

From the collection of Dick and Pat Spencer

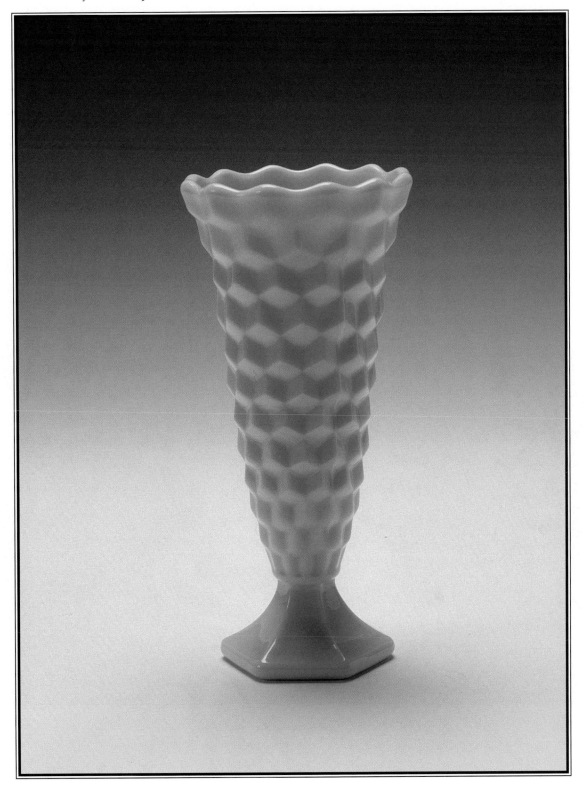

AMERICAN Milk blue vase – rare color

From the collection of Max Miller

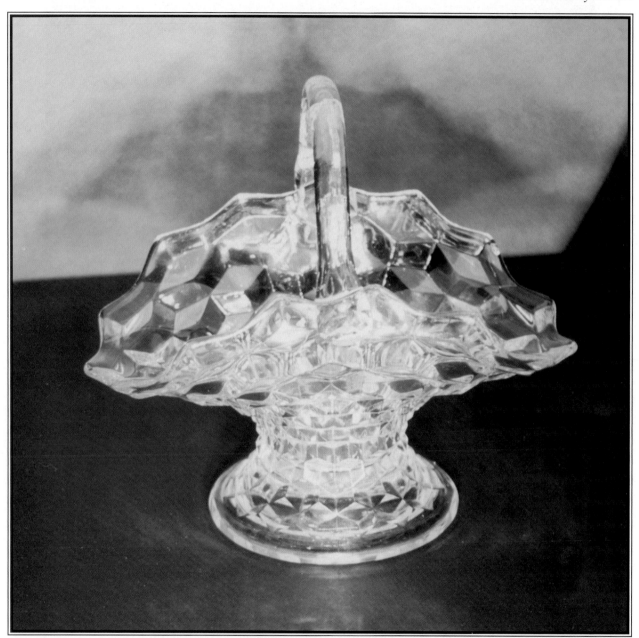

AMERICAN Crystal basket – rare item

From the collection of Kevin and Barbara Kiley

AMERICAN Crystal vase whimsy made from tumbler – rare item

From the collection of Earl and Beverly Hines

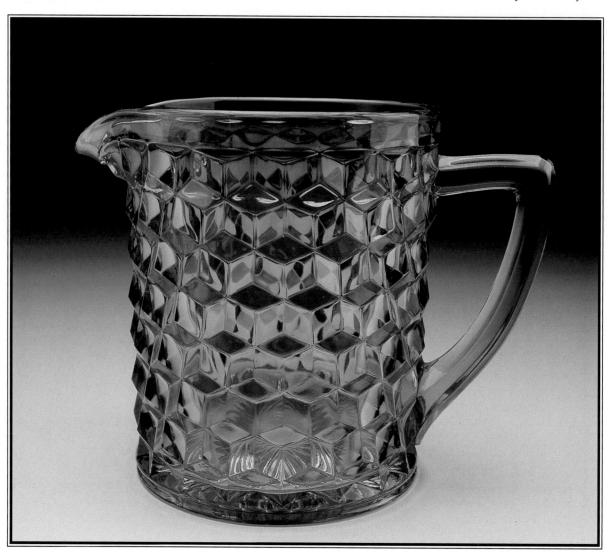

AMERICAN Green pitcher – rare color

From the collection of Kevin and Barbara Kiley

From the collection of Kevin and Barbara Kiley

*AMERICAN Opaque blue-green footed tumbler –
unusual color*

*AMERICAN Opaque speckled white footed tumbler –
unusual color*

From the collection of Sandy Hilterbran

CHINTZ *crystal dinner bell – rare item*

From the collection of Bruce Leslie

CHINTZ *crystal cigarette box – rare item*

From the collection of Dick and Pat Spencer

JAMESTOWN Green cake salver, 7" high, 10" diameter – rare color

Author's Collection

JUNE Pink footed oil bottle – rare item

From the collection of Ralph and Fran Leslie

NAVARRE Crystal bell – rare item
This bell is dated 1979 and was made for Avon.

Author's Collection

VESPER Amber egg cup – rare item

HAZEL-ATLAS GLASS COMPANY 1902–1956

Hazel-Atlas was formed from the merger of Hazel Glass Company and Atlas Glass and Metal Company in 1902. Containers and tumblers were their main wares until the Depression years. In the 1930s, starting with kitchenware items such as colored mixing bowls, they quickly branched into dinnerware patterns.

The Shirley Temple bowl, mug and milk pitcher that are recognized by almost everyone were made by Hazel-Atlas. Sets of Royal Lace and Moderntone in Ritz blue (cobalt) were advertised together for the same price: 44 pieces for $2.99! There is a huge price disparity between those patterns today!

In recent years, it has been the kitchenware and children's sets made by Hazel-Atlas that have come to the forefront. Collectors have eagerly gathered cobalt blue and pink sets of Criss Cross, as well as reamers and measuring cups. Pastel Moderntone children's sets from the late 1940s and early 1950s have skyrocketed in price of late. Many sets are difficult to find, but the solid white one shown below may be the creme de la creme!

From the collection of Jackie Morgan

MODERNTONE 16 piece white child's set in box – rare color

A.H. HEISEY & COMPANY 1896–1957

A.H. Heisey & Company opened its door in 1896. Their handsome pressed glassware was a success. In fact, the innovative idea of advertising glassware in national publications is attributed to Heisey. Glass was made continuously at the plant site in Newark, Ohio, until 1957. As with Cambridge, the glassware made in the 1930s to 1950s is the most collectible today.

One of the most difficult problems facing new collectors comes from the fact that the Heisey moulds were bought by Imperial in 1958, and many pieces were made at that plant until its demise in 1984. New collectors have to learn the Imperial colors because some of these pieces made by Imperial are similar to rare Heisey colors. Crystal pieces are more difficult to distinguish and collectors are beginning to accept this fact. Almost all of those Heisey/Imperial moulds were repurchased by the Heisey Collectors of America, Inc. and are now back in Newark, Ohio. So, there should be no danger of reissues being made from these moulds again.

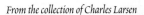

From the collection of Charles Larsen

COBALT Jamestown water goblet – rare color

From the collection of Gary and Sue Clark

CRYSTOLITE Crystal cocktail shaker – rare item

From the collection of Dick and Pat Spencer

IPSWICH Moongleam candlestick, footed with vase, "A" prisms – rare item

From the collection of Dick and Pat Spencer

OLD SANDWICH Moongleam cup and saucer – rare item
Very few of these cups and saucers have ever been
found in Moongleam.

Author's Collection

OLD SANDWICH Flamingo creamer – rare item

From the collection of Dick and Pat Spencer

ORCHID Crystal 14″ bowl – rare item

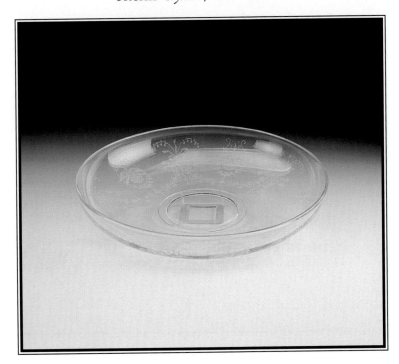

Author's Collection

ORCHID Crystal #4205 8″ bud vase – rare item

From the collection of Dick and Pat Spencer

RIDGELEIGH Crystal 6", 12 oz. tumbler – rare item
This newly discovered tumbler has a coaster bottom and a cupped in top!

Author's Collection

ROSE Crystal Universal cocktail icer – rare item

From the collection of Dick and Pat Spencer

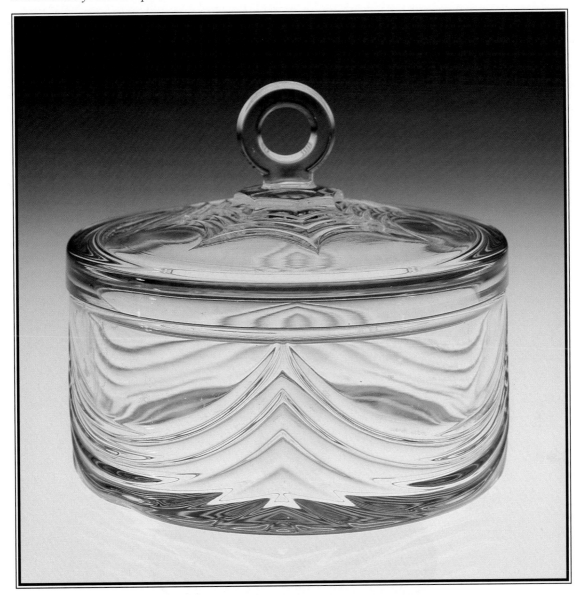

STANHOPE Crystal candy dish and cover – rare item

From the collection of Charles Larsen

YEOMAN Amber sherbet – rare color

HOCKING GLASS COMPANY 1905 to Present

Hocking became today's Anchor-Hocking in 1937, but most of the glassware pictured in this section was made before that merger. Several employees at Anchor-Hocking have gone out of their way to help me in my research in the twenty-three years I have been writing. They have also been at pains to protect the collectability of their older products by making noticeable changes in any similar reissued wares. Some companies have long since folded, but Anchor-Hocking is still meeting the consumer's needs!

Author's Collection

BLOCK OPTIC Green 3½" wine goblet – rare item
*Although I found a pink one of these about ten years ago, this green one only made its presence
known in 1994! This makes the known fifteen or twenty Cameo short wines seem common!*

Author's Collection

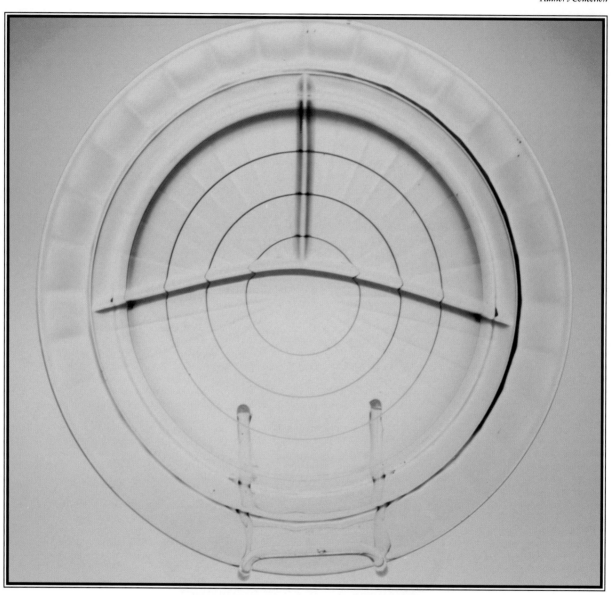

BLOCK OPTIC Green 10½" grill plate – rare item
Note that this plate has concentric rings and is paneled as is the dinner plate. There are other grill plates being passed as Block Optic; but these rarely found pieces have to have both characteristics to be Block!

Author's Collection

BLOCK OPTIC Green 5¾" blown vase – rare item

From the collection of Dan Tucker and Lorrie Kitchen

CAMEO Pink 3½" wine goblet – rare item
Rarely seen in green, these are even rarer in pink!

From the collection of Dan Tucker and Lorrie Kitchen

CAMEO Pink 7¼" salad bowl – rare item

From the collection of Dan Tucker and Lorrie Kitchen

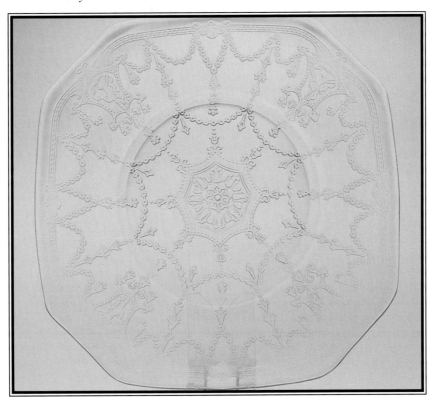

CAMEO Yellow 8½" square luncheon plate – rare item

Author's Collection

COLONIAL Green 7¾" beaded top pitcher without ice lip – rare item

Author's Collection

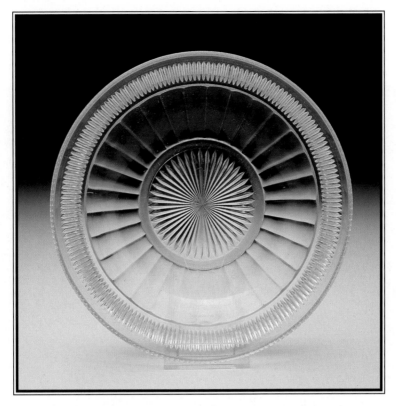

CORONATION Green 8½" luncheon plate – rare color

From the collection of Dan Tucker and Lorrie Kitchen

FIRE-KING DINNERWARE "JANE RAY" Green 9" flat soup – rare item

From the collection of Earl and Beverly Hines

FIRE-KING DINNERWARE "PHILBE" Blue 6", 36 oz. juice pitcher – rare item

From the collection of Earl and Beverly Hines

FIRE-KING DINNERWARE "PHILBE" Blue 4″, 9 oz. water tumbler – rare item

From the collection of Earl and Beverly Hines

FIRE-KING DINNERWARE "PHILBE" Green 3½" footed juice – rare item

From the collection of Earl and Beverly Hines

FIRE-KING DINNERWARE "PHILBE" Green 6", 36 oz. juice pitcher – rare item

FIRE-KING OVEN GLASS Sapphire blue whimsy – rare item
This piece was one of several whimsies that turned up recently. I had promises of pictures of some of the other items, but they were not forthcoming; so you will have to settle for this one piece made from the rectangular refrigerator dish.

Author's Collection

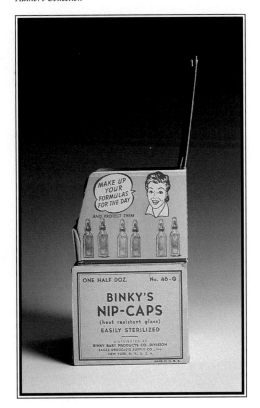

FIRE-KING OVEN GLASS Sapphire blue nipple cover – rare item
This original box of six Binky's Nip Caps was found in a Rhode Island consignment
shop several years ago for $2.00. I had only seen three of these nipple covers previously!

Author's Collection

FIRE-KING OVENWARE, TURQUOISE BLUE *batter bowl – rare item*
We hunted for years for this piece when collecting this pattern. This was spotted in
Nashville. I have only seen one other!

From the collection of Dick and Pat Spencer

HOCKING *"MAYFAIR" blue batter bowl – rare color*

From the collection of Dan Tucker & Lorrie Kitchen

MAYFAIR Crystal, footed, flared vase – rare item

From the collection of Dan Tucker & Lorrie Kitchen

MAYFAIR *Pink 5¼", 4½ oz., claret – rare item*

From the collection of Dan Tucker & Lorrie Kitchen

MAYFAIR *Pink round cups – rare items*
*This shows both style cups. The one on the left is thin and the one on the right is
thick. You can best see the differences at the center point where they are closest to each other.*

From the collection of Dan Tucker & Lorrie Kitchen

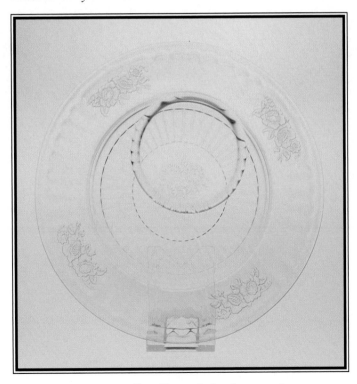

MAYFAIR *Yellow off center sherbet plate – rare item*

From the collection of Dan Tucker & Lorrie Kitchen

MAYFAIR Yellow 10" covered bowl – rare item

Author's Collection

*MISS AMERICA Royal Ruby 3¾", 3 oz. wine goblet
– rare color*

Author's Collection

*MISS AMERICA Royal Ruby 8" curved in bowl
– rare color*

Author's Collection

MISS AMERICA Royal Ruby 4¾", 5 oz. juice goblet – rare color
Notice the two different styles. The flared top juice is actually ¼" shorter than the regularly found straight side one.
The flared style has only been seen in red!

Author's Collection

OLD COLONY "LACE EDGE" 3½", 5 oz., flat juice – rare item
The juice is pictured beside the larger water so you can ascertain the difference.

Author's Collection

OLD COLONY "LACE EDGE" 9" comport – rare item
Notice the rayed bottom on the comport. Plain bottom comports were not made by Hocking.

From the collection of Dan Tucker & Lorrie Kitchen

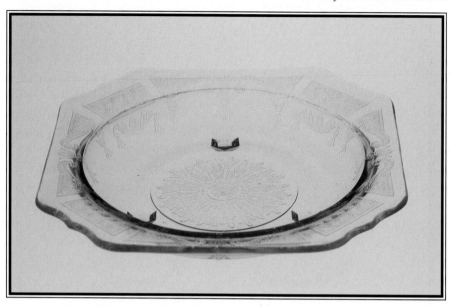

PRINCESS pink 8¾", square, three-footed relish – rare item

Author's Collection

SANDWICH Crystal 7½" scalloped bowl – rare item

From the collection of Dan Tucker & Lorrie Kitchen

PRINCESS Blue cookie jar – rare color

IMPERIAL GLASS CORPORATION 1904–1984

Although glass making began at Imperial in 1904, it was the start of a new era in 1936 when Candlewick was introduced. Until the company's demise in 1984, Imperial turned out a multitude of pieces in this pattern; but it was not their only pattern.

Author's Collection

BEADED BLOCK Canary yellow "pear" covered candy – rare item

From the collection of Dan Tucker & Lorrie Kitchen

CANDLEWICK Crystal banana stand with beaded edge – rare item

From the collection of Dan Tucker & Lorrie Kitchen

CANDLEWICK Crystal banana stand with pointed edge – rare item

From the collection of Dan Tucker & Lorrie Kitchen

CANDLEWICK Crystal 6½" basket – rare item
Both a side and end view are shown so you can see the edges.

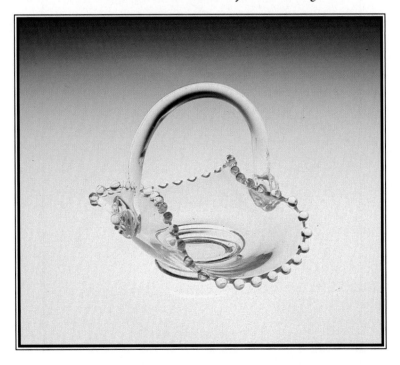

From the collection of Dan Tucker & Lorrie Kitchen

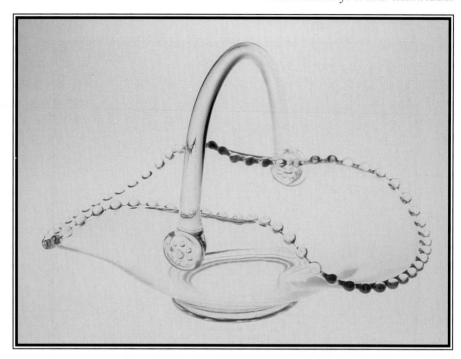

CANDLEWICK Crystal 11½" basket – rare item
Both a side and end view are shown so you can see the edges.

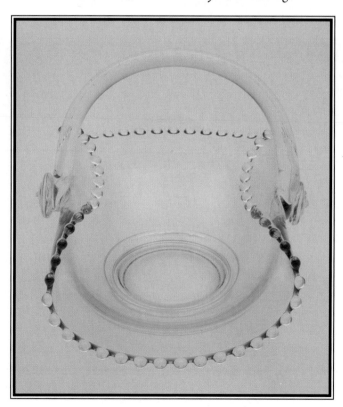

From the collection of Dan Tucker & Lorrie Kitchen

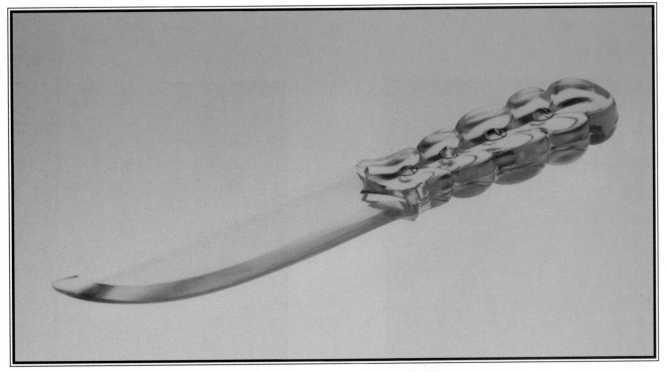

CANDLEWICK Crystal knife – rare item

Author's Collection

DIAMOND QUILTED Pink candlestick – rare item
*The normally found candlestick was altered at the factory to
make this whimsy.*

Author's Collection

CAPE COD Crystal whimsy vase made from a tumbler – rare item
Shown are two views of this vase so you can see the unusual top!

Indiana Glass has caused concern for collectors for years with their "re-issues." A more proper term might be reproductions! It is a shame because many pieces of their glass fit the "rare" category.

Author's Collection

AVOCADO White pitcher – rare color

Author's Collection

AVOCADO White tumbler – rare color

Author's Collection

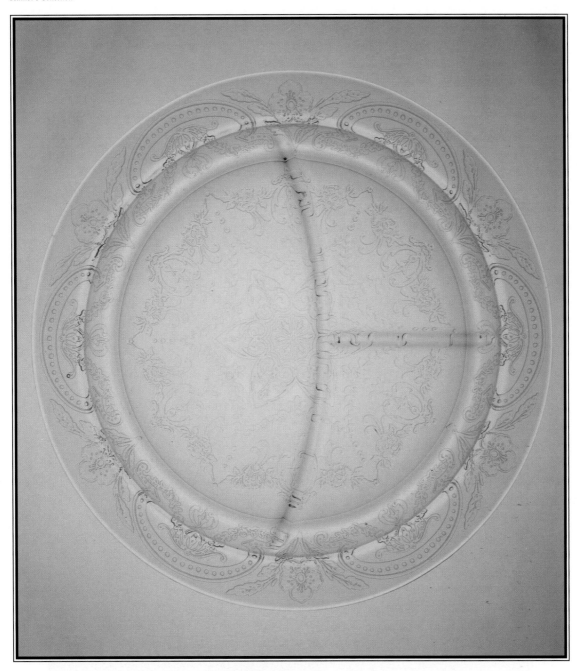

NO. 612 green 10⅜" grill plate – rare item

From the collection of Steve Nadort

OLD ENGLISH Pink pitcher – rare color

From the collection of Steve Nadort

OLD ENGLISH Pink 4½" and 5½" footed tumblers – rare color

Jeannette Glass Company seemed to have an affinity for making odd-colored glass from their standard glassware lines. Canary yellow (vaseline), red or even Delphite blue turns up in patterns once in a while. What makes this fact even more astounding is that those colors were not part of their repertoire in other patterns either. It's as if they wanted to cause us wonderment years later.

Author's Collection

ANNIVERSARY Shell Pink cake plate – rare item

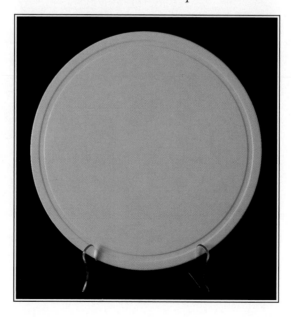

Author's Collection

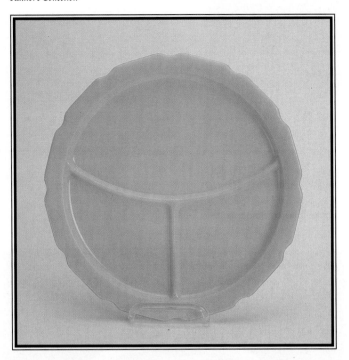

CHERRY BLOSSOM *Jadite grill plate – rare color*

Author's Collection

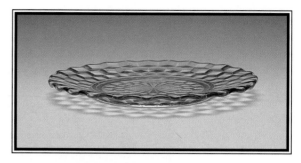

CUBE Green 8″ ruffled plate – rare item
Shown are two views so you can see the ruffling effect.

Author's Collection

CUBE Pink tab handled berry bowl – rare item
Although this bowl looks like a plate since it was set on its edge for photography purposes, it is a 6½″ bowl.
You will also find this same moulded bowl in Jeannette's Windsor pattern.

Author's Collection

CUBE Blue powder jar – rare color

Author's Collection

FLORAGOLD Iridescent 5½" square butter dish – rare item
Pictured are both sizes of square Floragold butter dishes. The 5½" butter is on the left and the normally found 6¼" is on the right.
Notice the top knob on the smaller butter. It is flat and not pointed! Only one of these smaller butters has ever been found!

From the collection of Dan Tucker and Lorrie Kitchen

FLORAL Cremax creamer – rare color

From the collection of Dan Tucker and Lorrie Kitchen

FLORAL Cremax sugar – rare color

From the collection of Dan Tucker and Lorrie Kitchen

FLORAL Cremax butter dish – rare color

From the collection of Dan Tucker and Lorrie Kitchen

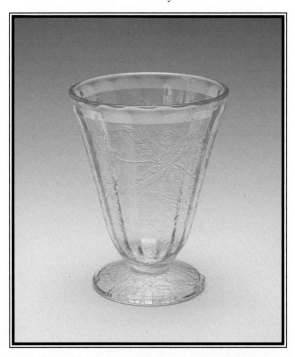

FLORAL Green 4¾", 6 oz., footed tumbler – rare item

Author's Collection

FLORAL Pink 7½" ruffled berry bowl – rare item

From the collection of Dan Tucker and Lorrie Kitchen

FLORAL Opaque red 8" berry bowl — rare color
Pattern has been highlighted (in the bottom photograph) in order for you to see it.

Author's Collection

HEX OPTIC Pink 8″, 96 oz., flat pitcher – rare item
Notice that this pitcher is very heavy as is the cone shaped style.
Those pitchers that are similar in shape but very thin were not made by Jeannette!

From the collection of Bill and Lottie Porter

From the collection of Bill and Lottie Porter

IRIS Flashed amethyst demitasse cup and saucer – rare color

IRIS Flashed blue demitasse cup and saucer – rare color

From the collection of Victor Elliot

IRIS Green creamer – rare color
This creamer was found in the Carolinas several years ago. I had a couple of reports of
another one having been seen in California, but that sighting was never confirmed!

From the collection of Bill and Lottie Porter

IRIS Iridescent demitasse cup and saucer – rare color

From the collection of Bettie's Cupboard/Orphan Annie's

IRIS Iridescent 5½", 4 oz., goblet – rare color
The lady who bought this goblet left the chipped one with
its $8.00 price tag!

From the collection of Bill and Lottie Porter

IRIS Flashed red demitasse cup and saucer – rare color

From the collection of Bill and Lottie Porter

SUNFLOWER Opaque beige cup – rare color
If anyone ever sees the matching saucer to this cup, please let me know!

Author's Collection

WINDSOR Transparent blue creamer – rare color

Author's Collection

WINDSOR Transparent blue tumbler – rare color

LANCASTER GLASS COMPANY 1908–1937

Although purchased by Hocking in 1924, Lancaster Glass of Lancaster, Ohio, continued under that name until 1937 when Hocking eliminated the name completely. This plant still operates today as plant #2 of Anchor-Hocking.

Author's Collection

JUBILEE Yellow 13" three-footed bowl – rare item

From the collection of Morris Antiques

JUBILEE Yellow 3", 8 oz., sherbet – rare item

Author's Collection

JUBILEE Yellow 7½", 11 oz., water goblet – rare item

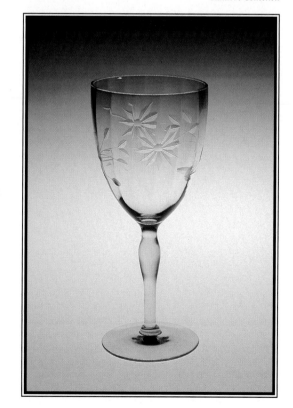

Author's Collection

JUBILEE Yellow 4¾", 4 oz., oyster cocktail – rare item

Author's Collection

PATRICK Pink 4¾" sherbet – rare item

LIBERTY GLASS WORKS 1903–1932

Located in New Jersey instead of the Ohio-Pennsylvania-West Virginia glass making triangle, this company prospered during the early days of Depression glass until a fire destroyed the plant and it was never rebuilt. They made many utilitarian items and provided us with one of the few dresser sets in pressed ware of the Depression era.

From the collection of Earl and Beverly Hines

AMERICAN PIONEER Amber covered urns – rare color
This is one of the few pairs of urns known.

MacBeth-Evans made some of the more popular Depression glass patterns, but as in competitors' products, some pieces are scarcely found today.

From the collection of Dan Tucker and Lorrie Kitchen

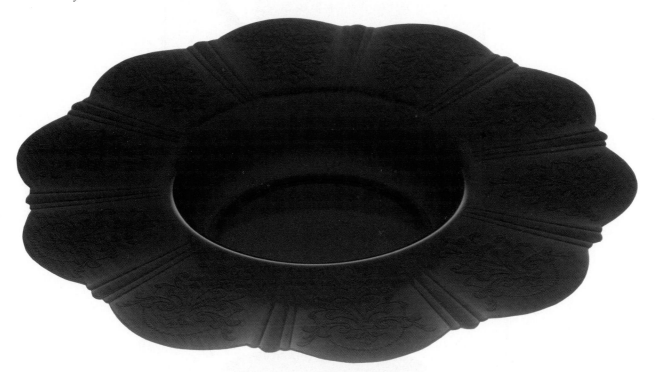

AMERICAN SWEETHEART Cobalt blue 18" console bowl – rare item

From the collection of Dan Tucker and Lorrie Kitchen

*AMERICAN SWEETHEART Metallic finish applied over cobalt creamer
– rare item
I was really surprised to see this technique used, especially over cobalt blue.*

From the collection of Dan Tucker and Lorrie Kitchen

AMERICAN SWEETHEART Metallic finish applied over cobalt sugar – rare item

From the collection of Dan Tucker and Lorrie Kitchen

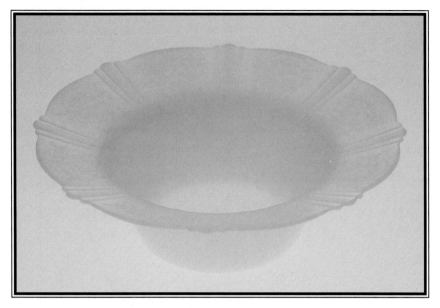

AMERICAN SWEETHEART Monax 6½" miniature console bowl — rare item

Author's Collection

DOGWOOD Crystal juice tumbler — rare color and item
I found five of these in an antique mall in Florida, but they are
the only ones I have ever seen. It was a pleasant surprise, but I
wish they had been pink!

From the collection of Dan Tucker and Lorrie Kitchen

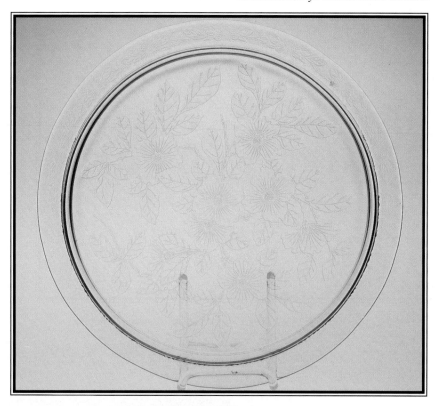

DOGWOOD *Pink 11" cake plate – rare item*
This piece first turned up at a Depression glass show in Cincinnati years ago. As far as I know,
no others have ever been found.

Author's Collection

PETALWARE *Monax Florette decorated 7" soup – rare item*
Obtaining Petalware soups is difficult enough, but to discover decorated ones was quite a
find in Pennsylvania last year.

McKEE GLASS COMPANY 1853–1951

The company was originally founded as McKee & Brothers Glass Works at Pittsburgh in 1853. It moved to a site east of Pittsburgh in Westmoreland County in 1888 and built its new plant there. This site became the town of Jeannette. The move from Pittsburgh had been necessitated by the availability of natural gas in the area of Jeannette. Later, with the depletion of this natural gas, the company turned to the other readily available fuel in the area – coal. McKee continued making glass at this site until 1951 when the Thatcher Glass Company bought the company.

When McKee is mentioned today, two things seem to stand out in collector's minds: Rock Crystal and kitchenware items. Collectors of Depression patterns immediately think of the red or crystal Rock Crystal pattern that was made from the early 1900s until the 1940s.

Author's Collection

ROCK CRYSTAL Red 8½" center handled bowl – rare item

Author's Collection

ROCK CRYSTAL Red syrup pitcher – rare item
When I received a call from Pittsburgh about this syrup, I found it hard to believe it existed since this particular item should have
been discontinued long before red was made. Evidently red was made before the known 1927 date listed elsewhere.

Author's Collection

ROCK CRYSTAL *Jap blue satinized 8" candlestick – rare color*
Jap blue was the name McKee gave to their blue color in the late 1920s. Many times this
blue and amethyst were satinized by applying camphoric acid.

From the collection of Kevin and Barbara Kiley

ROCK CRYSTAL Amber fluted 12½" footed center bowl – rare item
Bowl is shown from two views to show the fluting.

MORGANTOWN GLASS WORKS 1929–1972

First established in Morgantown, West Virginia, as Morgantown Glass Works, it became the Economy Glass Tumbler Co. in the early 1900s until 1929 when it again became Morgantown. It continued as Morgantown until bought out by Bailey Glass in 1972.

Author's Collection

SUNRISE MEDALLION "DANCING GIRL" blue pitcher – rare item
More of these have been found in the northwestern part of the country than anywhere else, although the very first one was found at Washington Court House, Ohio, in the early 1970s.

Author's Collection

SUNRISE MEDALLION "DANCING GIRL"
blue 2⁷⁄₁₆"-2⁹⁄₁₆", 4 oz. tumbler – rare item
Although these have been recorded as oyster cocktails, I am inclined to believe egg
cups would be a better term. Two of these are shown from the bottom so that you
can see how much variance there can be with hand made glassware.
(No, the smaller one has not been ground or polished!)

Author's Collection

SUNRISE MEDALLION "DANCING GIRL" pink sugar bowl – rare item
As with the green sugar pictured in third edition Very Rare, I am searching for the creamer to match.

Author's Collection

SUNRISE MEDALLION "DANCING GIRL" pink 6" vase – rare item
Notice the pink color variations between this vase and the sugar bowl pictured on the preceding page.

NEW MARTINSVILLE GLASS MANUFACTURING COMPANY

1901–1944

The factory became Viking Glass Company in 1944 and is still in operation today. Although they produced a multitude of colors during the Depression era, New Martinsville exhibited quality color control and were renowned for their Ruby (red) and their Ritz blue (cobalt blue).

Author's Collection

MOONDROPS Black tumbler – rare color

Author's Collection

MOONDROPS Pink "rocket" decanter – rare item

From the collection of Dick and Pat Spencer

MOONDROPS Ritz blue 9¾" covered casserole – rare item

Author's Collection

MOONDROPS Ruby cream soup – rare item

From the collection of Dick and Pat Spencer

RADIANCE Ruby punch set – rare item
Set with twelve cups and ladle

PADEN CITY GLASS COMPANY 1916–1951

Paden City Glass Company built its factory and started producing glassware all within a one-year time period. That was considered quite a feat in 1916. We think of Paden City as a company which produced a multitude of colors and made a variety of patterns containing birds. This handmade glass was not turned out in the large quantities that many of the glass factories of that day produced. Hence, items manufactured by Paden City are even more scarce 50 years later. Most of the glassware made by this company is exceedingly attractive in design.

From the collection of Bill and Lottie Porter

BLACK FOREST Gold encrusted cobalt blue pitcher – rare item

Author's Collection

CUPID Pink, gold decorated, flat sugar – rare item

Author's Collection

CUPID Pink, gold decorated, flat creamer – rare item
Two views are shown so you can see how the top of the Cupid decoration was moved to the sides to match the sugar. That moves the gold away
from the spout which saves additional wear to the gold!

From the collection of Kevin and Barbara Kiley

CROW'S FOOT *Red gravy and 10¾" oval fluted bowl
– rare items
The oval fluted bowl was so similar to the gravy that we
pictured them both so you could see the similarities.*

Author's Collection

NORA BIRD *Green tray – rare item*
Although photographed with the birds upside down, the photograph has been turned around so that they are not sitting on their heads!

From the collection of Bill and Millie Downey

CROW'S FOOT Red punch bowl set — rare item

Author's Collection

"PEACOCK REVERSE" Red 6½" square candy – rare item

Author's Collection

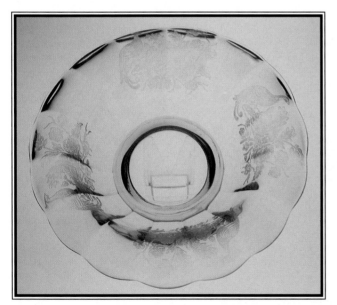
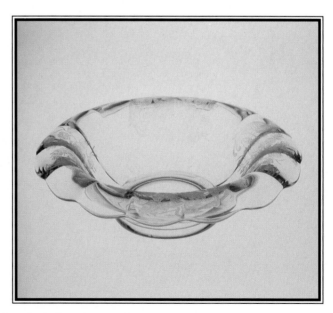

PEACOCK & WILD ROSE Blue 11" console bowl – rare color
This is the only piece of this pattern I have seen in this light blue.

The "R" factory of the U.S. Glass Company was located at Tiffin, Ohio. It was better known as the Tiffin Glass Co.

Author's Collection

CHEROKEE ROSE Crystal icer – rare item

Author's Collection

CLASSIC Pink footed pitcher – rare color

Author's Collection

Author's Collection

Above:
FLANDERS Pink consommé – rare item

Left:
FLANDERS Pink nut cup – rare item

Author's Collection

Author's Collection

Above:
FLANDERS Pink round covered flat candy
– rare item

Right:
FUCHSIA Crystal cup and saucer
– rare item

Author's Collection

FUCHSIA Crystal 12″ Chinese hurricane – rare item

The U. S. Glass Company was founded in 1891 as a merger of eighteen smaller companies in Ohio, Pennsylvania and West Virginia. Tiffin Glass Company was the "R" factory in this merger of smaller companies. While Flower Garden with Butterflies remains the most popular pattern collected from U.S. Glass, other patterns are beginning to attract many admirers.

Author's Collection

FLOWER GARDEN WITH BUTTERFLIES Blue 6" candy with green knob – rare color
This is the only two-color piece known in this pattern.

From the collection of Dan Tucker and Lorrie Kitchen

FLOWER GARDEN WITH BUTTERFLIES Black cologne bottle – rare color

Author's Collection

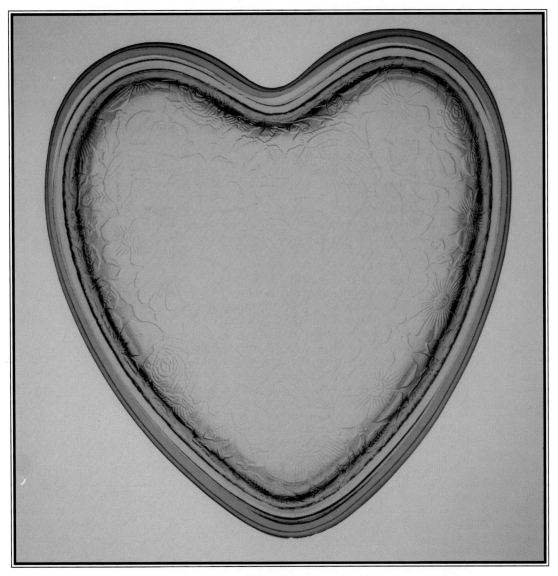

FLOWER GARDEN WITH BUTTERFLIES *Green heart shaped candy – rare item*
Only two green heart candies have surfaced, making this the rarest color found in these rarely seen pieces!

Started in 1890, in Grapeville, Pennsylvania, as the "Westmoreland Specialty Company," this company is better known by today's collectors for its milk glass productions than many of its numerous other glassware productions.

Author's Collection

ENGLISH HOBNAIL *Pink flat shaker – rare item*
Footed shakers abound in English Hobnail, but flat ones are scarce.

Author's Collection

ENGLISH HOBNAIL Crystal icer with patterned insert – rare item

Author's Collection

PANELED GRAPE Milk glass three piece epergne set – rare item
The epergne vase in this set is the hard to find part.

From the collection of Dan Tucker and Lorrie Kitchen

Black straw jar – rare color

From the collection of Dan Tucker and Lorrie Kitchen

Cobalt blue sugar shaker – rare color
This shaker is reminiscent of New Martinsville with its tripod foot.

VALUE GUIDE

Page 52
ROSE *Crystal Universal cocktail icer – $225.00-250.00*

Page 53
STANHOPE *Crystal candy dish and cover – $175.00-200.00*

Page 54
YEOMAN *Amber sherbet – $125.00-150.00*

Page 55
BLOCK OPTIC *Green 3½" wine goblet – $400.00-450.00*

Page 56
BLOCK OPTIC *Green 10½" grill plate – $20.00-30.00*

Page 57
BLOCK OPTIC *Green 5¾" blown vase – $275.00-300.00*

Page 58
CAMEO *Pink 3½" wine goblet – $750.00-850.00*

Page 59
CAMEO *Pink 7¼" salad bowl – $125.00-150.00*
CAMEO *Yellow 8½" square luncheon plate – $200.00-225.00*

Page 60
COLONIAL *Green 7¾" beaded top pitcher without ice lip – $900.00-1,000.00*

Page 61
CORONATION *Green 8½" luncheon plate – $35.00-40.00*
FIRE-KING DINNERWARE *"JANE RAY" Green 9" flat soup – $20.00-25.00*

Page 62
FIRE-KING DINNERWARE *"PHILBE" Blue 6", 36 oz. pitcher – $850.00-900.00*

Page 63
FIRE-KING DINNERWARE *"PHILBE"*
  Blue 4", 9 oz, water tumbler – $130.00-150.00

Page 64
FIRE-KING DINNERWARE *"PHILBE" Green 3½" footed juice – $150.00-175.00*

Page 65
FIRE-KING DINNERWARE *"PHILBE" Green 6", 36 oz. pitcher – $650.00-700.00*

Page 66
FIRE-KING OVEN GLASS *Sapphire blue whimsy – $125.00-150.00*

Page 67
FIRE-KING OVEN GLASS
  Sapphire blue nipple cover – $1,000.00-1,250.00 boxed set

Page 68
FIRE-KING OVENWARE *Turquoise blue batter bowl – $125.00-150.00*
HOCKING *"MAYFAIR" blue batter bowl – $125.00-150.00*

Page 69
MAYFAIR *Crystal, footed, flared vase – $1,500.00-1,750.00*

Page 70
MAYFAIR *Pink 5¼", 4½" claret – $900.00-1,000.00*

Page 71
MAYFAIR *Pink round cups – $300.00-400.00 EA.*
MAYFAIR *Yellow off center sherbet plate – $110.00-125.00*

Page 72
MAYFAIR *Yellow 10" covered bowl – $900.00-1,000.00*

Page 73
MISS AMERICA *Royal Ruby 3¾", 3 oz. wine goblet – $235.00-250.00*
MISS AMERICA *Royal Ruby 8" curved in bowl – $375.00-400.00*

Page 74
MISS AMERICA *Royal Ruby 4¾", 5 oz. juice goblet – $235.00-250.00 EA.*

Page 75
OLD COLONY *"LACE EDGE" 3½", 5 oz., flat juice – $75.00-100.00*
OLD COLONY *"LACE EDGE" 9" comport – $700.00-750.00*

Page 76
PRINCESS *Pink 8¾", square, three-footed relish – $900.00-1,000.00*
SANDWICH *Crystal 7½" scalloped bowl – $100.00-125.00*

Page 77
PRINCESS *Blue cookie jar – $800.00-900.00*

Page 78
BEADED BLOCK *Canary yellow "pear" covered candy – $225.00-250.00*

Page 79
CANDLEWICK *Crystal banana stand with beaded edge – $1,000.00-1,200.00*

Page 80
CANDLEWICK *Crystal banana stand with pointed edge – $1,000.00-1,200.00*

Page 81
CANDLEWICK *Crystal 6½" basket – $225.00-275.00*

Page 82
CANDLEWICK *Crystal 11½" basket – $500.00-550.00*

Page 83
CANDLEWICK *Crystal knife – $200.00-250.00*
DIAMOND QUILTED *Pink candlestick – $35.00-50.00*

Page 84
CAPE COD *Crystal whimsy vase made from a tumbler – $500.00-550.00*

Page 85
AVOCADO *White pitcher – $400.00-425.00*

Page 86
AVOCADO *White tumbler – $35.00-40.00*

Page 87
NO. 612 *Green 10⅜" grill plate – $75.00-80.00*

Page 88
OLD ENGLISH *Pink pitcher – $150.00-175.00*

Page 89
OLD ENGLISH *Pink 4½" & 5½" footed tumblers; 4½" – $22-25; 5½" – $30.00-35.00*

Page 90
ANNIVERSARY *Shell Pink cake plate – $125.00-150.00*

Page 91
CHERRY BLOSSOM *Jadite grill plate – $65.00-75.00*

Page 92
CUBE *Green 8" ruffled plate – $25.00-30.00*
CUBE *Pink tab handled berry bowl – $100.00-125.00*

Page 93
CUBE *Blue powder jar – $175.00-200.00*
FLORAGOLD *Iridescent 5½" square butter dish – $675.00-700.00*

Page 94
FLORAL *Cremax creamer – $160.00-175.00*
FLORAL *Cremax sugar – $160.00-175.00*

Page 95
FLORAL *Cremax butter dish – $300.00-350.00*

Page 96
FLORAL *Green 4¾", 6 oz., footed tumbler – $125.00-150.00*
FLORAL *Pink 7½" ruffled berry bowl – $125.00-150.00*

Page 97
FLORAL *Opaque red 8" berry bowl – $300.00-350.00*

Page 98
HEX OPTIC *Pink 8", 96 oz., flat pitcher* – $200.00-225.00

Page 99
IRIS *Flashed amethyst demitasse cup and saucer* – $250.00-275.00
IRIS *Flashed blue demitasse cup and saucer* – $250.00-275.00
IRIS *Green creamer* – $75.00-100.00

Page 100
IRIS *Iridescent demitasse cup and saucer* – $250.00-275.00
IRIS *Iridescent 5½", 4 oz., goblet* – $100.00-125.00

Page 101
IRIS *Flashed red demitasse cup and saucer* – $250.00-275.00
SUNFLOWER *Opaque beige cup* – $40.00-50.00

Page 102
WINDSOR *Transparent blue creamer* – $60.00-75.00
WINDSOR *Transparent blue tumbler* – $60.00-75.00

Page 103
JUBILEE *Yellow 13" three-footed bowl* – $225.00-250.00

Page 104
JUBILEE *Yellow 3", 8 oz., sherbet* – $65.00-75.00
JUBILEE *Yellow 7½", 11 oz., water goblet* – $135.00-150.00

Page 105
JUBILEE *Yellow 4¾", 4 oz., oyster cocktail* – $75.00-85.00
PATRICK *Pink 4¾" sherbet* – $65.00-75.00

Page 106
AMERICAN PIONEER *Amber covered urns;*
    5" urn – $250.00-300.00; *7" urn* – $300.00-350.00

Page 107
AMERICAN SWEETHEART *Cobalt blue 18" console bowl* – $900.00-1,000.00

Page 108
AMERICAN SWEETHEART
    Metallic finish applied over cobalt creamer – $125.00-150.00
AMERICAN SWEETHEART
    Metallic finish applied over cobalt sugar – $125.00-150.00

Page 109
AMERICAN SWEETHEART *Monax 6½" mini console bowl* – $1,500.00-1,750.00
DOGWOOD *Crystal juice tumbler* – $50.00-55.00

Page 110
DOGWOOD *Pink 11" cake plate* – $500.00-550.00
PETALWARE *Monax Florette decorated 7" soup* – $70.00-75.00

Page 111
ROCK CRYSTAL *Red 8½" center handled bowl* – $135.00-150.00

Page 112
ROCK CRYSTAL *Red syrup pitcher* – $600.00-750.00

Page 113
ROCK CRYSTAL *Jap blue satinized 8" candlestick* – $50.00-55.00

Page 114
ROCK CRYSTAL *Amber fluted 12½" footed center bowl* – $300.00-350.00

Page 115
SUNRISE MEDALLION *"Dancing Girl" Blue pitcher* – $450.00-500.00

Page 116
SUNRISE MEDALLION *"Dancing Girl"*
    Blue 2⁷⁄₁₆"-2⁹⁄₁₆", 4 oz. tumbler – $100.00-125.00

Page 117
SUNRISE MEDALLION *"Dancing Girl" Pink sugar bowl* – $250.00-300.00

Page 118
SUNRISE MEDALLION *"Dancing Girl" Pink 6" vase* – $350.00-400.00

Page 119
MOONDROPS *Black tumbler* – $40.00-50.00

Page 120
MOONDROPS *Pink "rocket" decanter* – $300.00-350.00

Page 121
MOONDROPS *Ritz blue 9¾" covered casserole* – $150.00-175.00
MOONDROPS *Ruby cream soup* – $85.00-100.00

Page 122
RADIANCE *Ruby punch set* – $400.00-450.00

Page 123
BLACK FOREST *Gold encrusted cobalt blue pitcher* – $1,250.00-1,500.00

Page 124
CUPID *Pink, gold decorated, flat sugar* – $125.00-150.00
CUPID *Pink, gold decorated, flat creamer* – $125.00-150.00

Page 125
CROW'S FOOT *Red gravy and 10¾" oval fluted bowl;*
    Gravy – $100.00-110.00; *Bowl* – $175.00-200.00
NORA BIRD *Green tray* – $125.00-150.00

Page 126
CROW'S FOOT *Red punch bowl set* – $450.00-500.00

Page 127
"PEACOCK REVERSE" *Red 6½" square candy* – $135.00-150.00
PEACOCK & WILD ROSE *Blue 11" console bowl* – $75.00-100.00

Page 128
CHEROKEE ROSE *Crystal icer* – $70.00-75.00

Page 129
CLASSIC *Pink footed pitcher* – $350.00-400.00

Page 130
FLANDERS *Pink consommé* – $70.00-75.00
FLANDERS *Pink nut cup* – $60.00-65.00

Page 131
FLANDERS *Pink round covered flat candy* – $300.00-350.00
FUCHSIA *Crystal cup and saucer* – $65.00-75.00

Page 132
FUCHSIA *Crystal 12" Chinese hurricane* – $125.00-150.00

Page 133
FLOWER GARDEN WITH BUTTERFLIES
    Blue 6" candy with green knob – $125.00-150.00

Page 134
FLOWER GARDEN WITH BUTTERFLIES
    Black cologne bottle – $500.00-550.00

Page 135
FLOWER GARDEN WITH BUTTERFLIES
    Green heart shaped candy – $1,200.00-1,300.00

Page 136
ENGLISH HOBNAIL *Pink flat shaker* – $60.00-75.00

Page 137
ENGLISH HOBNAIL *Crystal icer with patterned insert* – $40.00-45.00

Page 138
PANELED GRAPE *Milk glass three piece epergne set* – $300.00-350.00

Page 139
Black straw jar – $600.00-750.00

Page 140
Cobalt blue sugar shaker – $700.00-750.00

Schroeder's ANTIQUES Price Guide

. . . is the #1 best-selling antiques & collectibles value guide on the market today, and here's why . . .

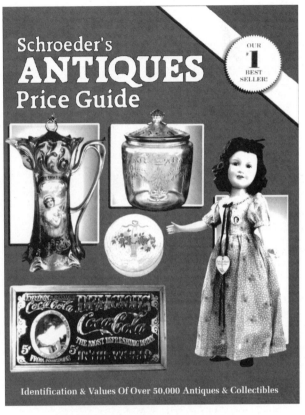

Schroeder's ANTIQUES Price Guide

OUR #1 BEST SELLER!

Identification & Values Of Over 50,000 Antiques & Collectibles

8½ x 11, 608 Pages, $12.95

• *More than 300 advisors, well-known dealers, and top-notch collectors work together with our editors to bring you accurate information regarding pricing and identification.*

• *More than 45,000 items in almost 500 categories are listed along with hundreds of sharp original photos that illustrate not only the rare and unusual, but the common, popular collectibles as well.*

• *Each large close-up shot shows important details clearly. Every subject is represented with histories and background information, a feature not found in any of our competitors' publications.*

• *Our editors keep abreast of newly developing trends, often adding several new categories a year as the need arises.*

If it merits the interest of today's collector, you'll find it in *Schroeder's*. And you can feel confident that the information we publish is up to date and accurate. Our advisors thoroughly check each category to spot inconsistencies, listings that may not be entirely reflective of market dealings, and lines too vague to be of merit. Only the best of the lot remains for publication.

Without doubt, you'll find
SCHROEDER'S ANTIQUES PRICE GUIDE
the only one to buy for
reliable information and values.

COLLECTOR BOOKS
A Division of Schroeder Publishing Co., Inc.